Living God's Word

Revised

A Workbook for Catechetical Helps

by Edwin A. Jiede

CONCORDIA PUBLISHING HOUSE · SAINT LOUIS

Project editors: Kenneth C. Wagener and Rodney L. Rathmann

7   8   9   10   11   12   13   14   15   16   12   11   10   09   08   07   06   05   04   03

 Introduction

A. The Catechism

Circle the "Y" (Yes) before true statements and the "N" (No) before false statements.

Y   N   1. Everything that we should know for our salvation is written in the Bible.

Y   N   2. Our Catechism contains the main teachings of the Bible.

Y   N   3. Any book which teaches God's Word to children is a Catechism.

Y   N   4. Luther found during a visitation of the churches that many people knew none of the important Bible teachings.

Y   N   5. Dr. Martin Luther lived about 400 years ago.

Y   N   6. Luther wrote his Small Catechism chiefly to help pastors learn the chief parts of Christian doctrine.

Y   N   7. Just as Moses and the prophets were inspired by God to write the Old Testament, so was Luther inspired to write the Catechism.

Y   N   8. The "Six Chief Parts" of the Catechism present the main teachings of the Bible.

B. The Bible

Make sentences by crossing out the words you do not need.

1. In our confirmation instruction we have time to study only the (New Testament—main teachings) of the Bible because the Bible is really a library of (39—66) books.

2. Since the Bible is (good literature—God's Word), it deserves to be called the (Book of books—law).

3. The Old Testament was written in (Greek—Hebrew—Latin) by (Moses and the prophets—evangelists and apostles).

4. The New Testament contains books known as (poetry—gospels—prophecy—history—law—epistles).

5. The Old Testament books point to the (Savior—law—apostles) while the New Testament books tell chiefly what the (apostles—Savior) did for sinners.

6. Although the writing was done by (human beings—God), the Bible is (a human—God's) Word because His Holy Spirit "breathed into" the writers (all—most—some) of the thoughts and words they wrote.

7. The Bible (contains—is) the Word of God.

C. The Use of the Bible

Circle the names of those who show proper respect for the Bible.

1. Alissa is eager to attend confirmation instruction classes.
2. Joshua's pastor had to remind him that those who attend confirmation instruction should attend church regularly.
3. Elizabeth's Bible has a place of honor on the center table and is dusted every Saturday.
4. Miguel enjoys hearing his father read a Bible story.
5. Jacob didn't grumble when he had to quit the basketball team to attend the instruction class.
6. Joanne saved her allowance to buy a new Bible.
7. Thomas didn't learn all the Bible passages he had been asked to memorize.
8. Kumiko decided to read the Bible through in three years by reading a chapter a day.

D. Law and Gospel

The two main doctrines of the Bible are the Law and the Gospel.
Place an "L" or a "G" before each statement to indicate whether it refers to Law or to Gospel.

_____ 1. Jesus suffered and died to save sinners.
_____ 2. The Ten Commandments tell us how God wants us to live.
_____ 3. The doctrine of sin is clearly shown in both Testaments.
_____ 4. God loves all people.
_____ 5. "Love your neighbor as yourself." Matthew 22:39
_____ 6. But the angel said to them, "Do not be afraid. I bring you good news of great joy that will be for all the people." Luke 2:10

E.

Write these words in the correct blank spaces:

hear	live	believe	Christ	Way
read	precious	heaven	study	

The Bible is the most _____ book because from it we learn the _____ that leads to _____. That Way is _____. Christians stay on the heavenly way as they _____, _____, _____, and _____ the Bible and _____ according to it.

F.

Learn to spell these words. Use as many as you can in two sentences.

catechism   testament   Gospel   Bible   inspiration   Martin Luther

1
The First Commandment

A. The Law

Number these statements in the correct time order.

_____ For the sake of clearness God found it necessary to give the Law a second time.

_____ The full will of God is made known to us in the Bible.

_____ The Law was written first into the human heart.

_____ Moses published the Law about 1500 B.C.

_____ Through sin the Law became blurred.

B.

List the four ways in which human beings may know that there is a God.

1. _____   3. _____

2. _____   4. _____

C. Attributes of God

Match the Facts with the Reasons.

Fact

_____ 1. God can help me in every trouble.

_____ 2. God is with me in every danger.

_____ 3. God hates to see me sin.

_____ 4. God is always kind to me.

_____ 5. God shows me more kindness than I deserve.

_____ 6. God is as loving now as He ever was.

_____ 7. God was never born or made nor will He ever die.

_____ 8. God has a right to punish the godless.

_____ 9. God knows all my thoughts.

_____ 10. God never breaks a promise.

_____ 11. God shows mercy to those who love Him.

_____ 12. I cannot see God.

Reason

a. God is holy.

b. God is unchangeable.

c. God is eternal.

d. God is omnipotent.

e. God is omniscient.

f. God is good.

g. God is faithful.

h. God is omnipresent.

i. God is a spirit.

j. God is merciful.

k. God is just.

l. God is gracious.

D. The Holy Trinity

Write these words and phrases in the proper order to form true statements describing the Holy Trinity. Supply punctuation. The first word in every statement is italicized.

1. three distinct, separate Persons   yet   *God* is one divine Essence

   _____

2. are equally God, eternal, and uncreated   they are only one God
   Although Father, Son, and Holy Spirit

   _____

3. is not one-third of God   *Each* Person of the Holy Trinity   the true God
   each one is

   _____

   _____

4. three in one, and one in three   beyond my understanding
   That God can be   is

   _____

   _____

E. Disobeying the First Commandment

In which way did each of these people sin against the First Commandment?

1. James worried when a black cat crossed his path.

   _____

2. Li put a quarter into the church offering plate and spent the rest of her weekly allowance—$10—at the mall that afternoon.

   _____

3. Sarah obeyed her mother and told the man at the door, "My mother isn't home."

   _____

4. When his friends taunted him for being a "sissy," Raul began to use curse words occasionally.

   _____

5. Mr. Thompson often misses church during summer to play golf.

   _____

F. Obeying the First Commandment

Think of one instance in which you can show proper FEAR of God "above all things"; an instance in which you can show proper LOVE for God "above all things"; an instance in which you can show TRUST in God "above all things."

   _____

   _____

   _____

G.

Learn to spell these words. Use as many as you can in two sentences.

eternal   omniscient   omnipotent   triune   omnipresent

2 The Second Commandment

A. Definitions

Draw a line from each word to the correct definition.

1. God's Name
2. Curse
3. Swear
4. Use satanic arts
5. Lie
6. Deceive by God's name
7. False oath
8. Blasphemous oath
9. Frivolous oath
10. Oath in uncertain things

call upon God to witness the truth of what you say and to punish you if you do not tell the truth.

teach false doctrine as the Word of God.

that by which He is called and known.

use religion as a cloak for hypocrisy.

speak evil of God; wish evil to ourselves or to others.

fortunetelling and the like.

swear to commit a sin.

swear to that of which you are not sure.

swear to a lie.

swear thoughtlessly.

B. Conclusions

If the three sentences lead to a correct conclusion, underscore the conclusion.
If the conclusion is incorrect, draw a line through it.

1. I dishonor God's name if I continually use it thoughtlessly.
   God's name is holy.
   God's name stands for Him.
   Therefore, if I continually use God's name thoughtlessly, I dishonor God Himself.
2. Words of praise spoken insincerely are meaningless.
   Words of thanks spoken thoughtlessly are useless.
   John curses habitually, without thinking what he says.
   Therefore, cursing is sin only if we really mean what we say.
3. Godless people do not care if they offend God openly.
   Godless people often use God's name in vain.
   Cursing is often a fruit of a godless life.
   Therefore, by cursing I give the impression that I am godless.

C.

Write the words that match the kind of sin involved in each statement. These words will apply: curse, false oath, blasphemous oath, frivolous oath, uncertain oath, satanic arts, lie, and deceive.

_____ 1. A pastor said, "Most of God's Word is true."

_____ 2. After the school picnic Charmion said to Alyce, "Honest to God, I never had so much fun in my life."

_____ 3. Keisha believed what the astrologer told her.

_____ 4. Neil testified in court regarding things of which he was not sure.

_____ 5. Marty misplayed the ball and said, "The d—n ball took a bad bounce."

_____ 6. Susan told a lie in court to help her father.

_____ 7. A dishonest salesman attended church regularly because many of his customers attended.

_____ 8. Meredith swore that she would hate her teacher as long as she lived.

D.

Complete these sentences:

1. In the past, many people bowed their heads at the n _ _ _ o_ J_ _ _ _ _.
2. Not to use God's name at all is a s_ _ o _ o_ _ _ _ _ _ _ _ _.
3. Many people who are quick to call on God's name in time of trouble are likely to forget calling on it in g _ _ _ d _ _ _.
4. It is easier to pray than to p _ _ _ _ _.
5. Many persons fail to thank because they do not t _ _ _ _.

E.

(A). List briefly three times when you called on God's name in good days.

1. _____

2. _____

3. _____

(B). List briefly three times when you praised God.

1. _____

2. _____

3. _____

Why are spiritual blessings of greater importance than material blessings?

F.

Learn to spell these words. Use as many as you can in two sentences.

satanic arts   curse   swear   commandment   doctrine   idolatry

3 The Third Commandment

A.

Follow the directions of each statement.

1. If Jesus told us to keep the seventh day holy, circle the first letter. If not, circle the second.   T   W

2. If one day of worship each week is the only time Christians may worship, circle the first letter. If not, circle the second.   E   O

3. If failing to worship God regularly is a sin, circle the first letter. If not, circle the second.   R   L

4. If church attendance is less important during summer vacation, circle the first letter. If not, circle the second.   L   S

5. If dreaming during the sermon deprives your soul of blessings, circle the first letter. If not, circle the second.   H   O

6. If every one who attends church is necessarily a believer, circle the first letter. If not, circle the second.   T   I

7. If hearing and learning God's Word cheerfully is God-pleasing, circle the first letter. If not, circle the second.   P   H

8. If it is right that you should live according to God's Word, circle the first letter. If not, circle the second.   G   E

9. If listening to a television or radio sermon is a good reason for missing church, circle the first letter. If not, circle the second.   R   O

10. If hearing God's Word without believing honors God, circle the first letter. If not, circle the second letter.   S   D

11. If giving time and money to support the church is our Christian calling, circle the exclamation mark. If not, circle the period.   !   .

B.

Circle the words which best complete each sentence.

1. God told the Israelites to worship publicly on (any—the first—the seventh) day of the week.

2. Jesus fixed for our public worship on (the first—the seventh—every—no particular) day of the week.

3. Sunday was chosen as a day of public worship by the early Christians, because Sunday was (a Roman holiday—the resurrection day of Jesus—the New Testament holy-day commanded by the Lord).

4. Sunday is chiefly a day for public worship, but God also wants us to use it as a day of (fasting—rest and recreation—refraining from all play and pleasure).

C.

Place a check (✓) in one of the three columns to indicate whether the Sunday activity is pleasing to God, permitted, or forbidden. Presuppose that in every instance the person has attended church, unless otherwise stated.

	Pleasing to God	Permitted	Forbidden
1. Say a silent prayer before, after, and during church.			
2. Play ball.			
3. Pray for an unchurched friend.			
4. Attend a violent, sexually explicit movie.			
5. Sing in the church choir.			
6. Criticize the pastor's sermon.			
7. Miss church to attend a picnic.			
8. Read the paper.			
9. Drink or eat to excess.			
10. Watch sports on television.			
11. Teach a Sunday school class.			
12. Participate in a church organization event.			
13. Repair a bicycle.			
14. Miss church to rest after being out late Saturday night.			
15. Visit with friends.			

D.

Cross out the word that doesn't belong in each group.
See Lutheran Worship, *pages 8–9, if necessary.*

1. Christmas Day—Easter Day—Pentecost—Reformation
2. Ash Wednesday—Advent—Palm Sunday—Maundy Thursday—Good Friday
3. Lent—Ascension—Pentecost—The Holy Trinity
4. Epiphany of our Lord—Christmas Eve—Transfiguration—Baptism of our Lord
5. St. Andrew, Apostle—Martin Luther, Doctor and Confessor—St. Michael and All Angels—Mission Festival

E.

Learn to spell these words. Use as many as you can in two sentences.

Sabbath   sanctify   worship   Trinity   Pentecost

4
The Fourth Commandment

A.

Choose the correct ending for the sentence-starters by writing the key letters on the line.

1. My neighbor is every one that _____
2. Even an enemy can _____
3. God rules us through His representatives _____
4. We need not obey our parents if they _____
5. The first three Commandments require _____
6. "Love toward all people" summarizes the _____

a. in home, church, school, and state.
b. love toward God.
c. be my neighbor.
d. is in need of love.
e. Second Table of the Law.
f. command us to do something contrary to God's will.

B.

Write yes after each statement that is true. Write no after each statement that is not true.

1. God wants me to be grateful for what my parents do for me. _____
2. A Christian must obey the government regardless of what the laws ask. _____
3. A 14-year old needs to obey his or her parents as much as a 6-year old child. _____
4. Fear and love for God prompt me to obey my parents. _____
5. Obedient children always live to a ripe old age. _____
6. Next to God, my parents are my dearest friends. _____
7. If I love my parents I will gladly serve them. _____
8. I sin if I cause my parents to worry. _____

C.

Use your Bible to match these truths with the correct Bible passage. Write Matthew 7:12; Colossians 3:20; Proverbs 30:17; 1 Peter 2:18; Romans 13:1; Hebrews 13:17; 1 Timothy 5:4; Leviticus 19:32; Acts 5:29; or Proverbs 23:22 before each truth.

_____ 1. God demands that we respect elderly persons.

_____ 2. Christian children please the Lord by obeying their parents.

_____ 3. Children should love and respect their aged parents.

_____ 4. Love others as much as you love yourself.

_____ 5. I must obey the government.

_____   6.   Children will be punished if they disobey or mock their parents.

_____   7.   Children should repay their parents with obedience, service, and love.

_____   8.   Employees should obey the reasonable demands of their employers.

_____   9.   We may disobey the government if a law commands a thing contrary to God's will.

_____   10.   I must respect and obey my teacher.

D.

Be prepared to tell this briefly:

1. What have your parents done for your life?

    a. Physical   _____

    b. Mental   _____

    c. Social   _____

    d. Spiritual   _____

2. Think of at least five ways in which you can serve your parents.

    a.   _____

    b.   _____

    c.   _____

    d.   _____

E.

Learn to spell these words. Use the three words in one sentence.

provoke   esteem   despise

5
The Fifth Commandment

A.

Write these words in the correct blank spaces.

Life	murder	safeguard	just
government	befriend	death	help
carelessness	self-defense	accidental	

1. A person's _____ is his or her most valuable earthly possession.
2. God gave the Fifth Commandment to _____ body and life.
3. Willfully to hate or hurt someone is a form of _____.
4. Actual murder may be punished with _____.
5. Only the _____ has the right to inflict capital punishment.
6. It is not murder to kill in _____ or in a _____ war.
7. _____ killing is not murder, but killing through _____ is serious.
8. I ought to _____ and _____ my neighbor in every physical need.

B. Three Forms of Murder

Tell which form of murder is involved in each case by writing the letters a *(Coarse),* b *(Finer),* or c *(Finest) before each sentence.*

_____ 1. Injure a child by riding a bicycle carelessly.
_____ 2. Have an abortion.
_____ 3. Cause your parents sleepless nights by being disobedient.
_____ 4. Commit suicide.
_____ 5. Hate the neighbor who won't let you walk across his lawn.
_____ 6. Drive an auto while intoxicated and kill a man.
_____ 7. Beat up a boy in a fight.
_____ 8. Never support a congregational ministry project with your offerings.
_____ 9. Grant a "painless death" to a person who is incurably sick in body or mind.
_____ 10. Ruin your health by keeping late hours and depriving yourself of sufficient sleep.

C.

Check (✓) the BEST explanation for the stated facts.

1. Deliberate murder is punishable with death because
   _____ God says so. (Matthew 26:52)
   _____ a murderer is a wicked person.
   _____ the punishment should fit the crime.

2. Quarreling is sinful because it

_____ shows bad manners.

_____ may lead to mean deeds.

_____ springs from a hateful heart.

3. By overworking, overeating, or exercising to excess we sin because

_____ we show lack of common sense.

_____ we try to show off.

_____ we thereby harm our body.

4. Causing someone unnecessary grief is sinful because

_____ we are being thoughtless.

_____ worry and anxiety shorten life.

_____ we have nothing to gain by doing so.

5. Suicide is a sin because

_____ it shows cowardice.

_____ it shows a lack of trust in God.

_____ it often leaves unanswered questions.

D.

Circle the names of those who truly kept the Fifth Commandment.

1. Samuel saved a part of his allowance for the collection his school was raising for the Feed the World program.
2. Katlyn slammed the door shut when a poor woman asked for a drink of water.
3. Janelle did the dishes for the sick lady downstairs.
4. The teacher made Jeffrey do extra work for not paying attention. Jeffrey said to himself, "I hate that teacher."
5. When Mrs. Williams was ill, her neighbor didn't offer to help with the housework. Now Mrs. Williams says, "Wait until she gets sick! See if I help her."
6. Lamont missed a ballgame in order to visit a sick classmate.
7. Courtney outgrew a good dress. She asked her mother if she could give it to the church clothing drive.
8. The boys shared their lunch with Jonathan, who had forgotten his.
9. Christine at times makes herself sick by eating too much candy.
10. Clayton rides his bicycle recklessly, at times not observing traffic signals.

E.

Write the correct number before each name to show how each of the Bible characters sinned against the Fifth Commandment.

_____ Cain

_____ David

_____ Pharaoh

_____ Joseph's brothers

_____ Esau

_____ Saul

_____ Jezebel

_____ Pilate

_____ The Levite

1. murdered baby boys.
2. would not help an injured man.
3. told lies to kill and steal.
4. killed his brother in cold blood.
5. pursued a man to kill him.
6. killed a man to get his wife.
7. wanted to kill his brother.
8. caused their father much grief.
9. condemned an innocent man to death.

F.

Learn to spell these words. Use as many as you can in two sentences.

befriend   physical   suicide   euthanasia   abortion

6 The Sixth Commandment

A.

Fill in fitting endings for these sentences.

1. To safeguard marriage and the home, and to promote purity,
   God gave the _____ _____.
2. Marriage was instituted by _____.
3. Marriage is a lifelong union formed by _____ and _____.
4. Husband and wife are to remain together as long as they both shall _____.
5. The only true grounds for divorce are _____.

B.

Read the sentence. Then underline the word that could be used in place of the italicized word.

1. The Sixth Commandment asks that we lead a *pure* life.
   active   diligent   decent
2. Our actions, words, and thoughts ought to be *proper*.
   intelligent   loving   careful
3. King David committed *sexual immorality* with Uriah's wife.
   lust   adultery   deception
4. God *ordained* marriage.
   sanctified   instituted   blessed
5. If a husband gives his love to another woman, his wife has just ground for *separation*.
   desertion   hatred   divorce

C.

Tell why each of these actions could lead to gross impurity.

1. Day dreaming
2. Looking at indecent pictures
3. Listening to filthy stories
4. Telling dirty stories
5. Watching indecent movies
6. Associating with sinful companions
7. Reading stories with immoral plots
8. Idling away time
9. Dressing scantily
10. Dancing

D.

Five aids in avoiding impurity are (a) God's Word, (b) prayer, (c) hard work and play,
(d) good companions and environment, and (e) moderation in all things.
Write a, b, c, d, or e before each statement to indicate which aid was used.

_____ 1. Alex threw away the pornographic magazine because he recalled the words, "Keep yourself pure."

_____ 2. Stephanie no longer associates with certain girls because they are sexually active.

_____ 3. Ryan played tennis and baseball a good deal during the summer to keep from day-dreaming.

_____ 4. Meagan made sure the movie was "clean" before going to see it.

_____ 5. Jessica didn't accept a date unless she was certain that the boy was a Christian.

_____ 6. Nicholas prayed, "Create in me a clean heart, O God!" as he went to bed each night.

_____ 7. Lindsey dressed sensibly rather than have the boys whistle at her.

_____ 8. Jeremy went to the Lord's Supper frequently.

_____ 9. Jason found himself day-dreaming; so he went out to repair his bicycle.

_____ 10. Kyle knew of some boys who did bad things in secret. He asked the Lord to give them clean hearts.

E.

Tell what is WRONG in each of these statements.

1. Marriage is merely a human custom. _____

_____

_____

2. Under no condition may a husband or wife ask for a divorce. _____

_____

_____

3. A dirty joke now and then won't hurt anyone. _____

_____

_____

4. All dancing is sinful. _____

_____

_____

F.

Learn to spell these words. Use as many of them as you can in three sentences.

adultery   spouse   immorality   chaste   divorce   marriage

The Seventh Commandment

A.

Make the sentences meaningful by crossing out the unnecessary words.

1. All (precious—earthly) things really belong to (God—us).
2. In our relationship to God, we are (stewards—owners) of our possessions.
3. In using (our—God's) possessions we use them for (God's—our own) purposes.
4. Everyone must (respect—love) the possessions of his (friends—neighbors).

B.

Stealing may take place directly or indirectly in various forms.
Write the word Robbery, Theft, Usury, Fraud, Covetousness, Envy, Partnership, Laziness,
or Robbing God *before each statement to indicate which form applies to the situation.*

_____ 1. Adam lent Amy $10 with the understanding that he would be repaid $15 the next day.

_____ 2. An escaped convict held up a filling station.

_____ 3. Christopher at times accompanies boys who steal apples out of an orchard.

_____ 4. Taylor has been known to use her offering for attending a movie.

_____ 5. A fruit dealer knew that there were bruised tomatoes at the bottom of the basket but he told the customer they were all good.

_____ 6. Tria bought a soda while shopping for her mother but did not say so when she gave back the change.

_____ 7. Michelle feels the urge to take a bottle of perfume. "If only the clerk were gone!" she says to herself.

_____ 8. Andrew is displeased because his friend, Jason, got a new bicycle.

_____ 9. Douglas is paid by the hour but spends a good deal of his time loafing at work.

C.

These sentences tell a story if arranged in the correct order. Show the correct order by writing 1, 2, 3, 4, and 5 in the appropriate blank.

_____ He places a portion of His money and goods into our possession.

_____ We are to use these loaned gifts as faithful stewards because on the Last Day we must give a report to God.

_____ God really owns all money and goods.

_____ Faithful stewards use God's gifts for supporting themselves, loved ones, the poor and needy, the church and missions.

_____ Misers, spendthrifts, idlers, gamblers, and those who give little or nothing to the church are unfaithful stewards.

D.

Write yes or no to indicate whether or not you could IMPROVE a neighbor's property or business in this way.

_____ 1. Recommend a good dentist to friends.

_____ 2. Be discourteous to customers while working at your job.

_____ 3. Thank your church organist.

_____ 4. Be loud and boisterous at the school assembly.

_____ 5. Take your dog into a store where dogs aren't allowed.

_____ 6. Shop at a store that offers good service.

_____ 7. Loaf at your job.

_____ 8. Fail to tell the clerk that he gave you too much change.

_____ 9. Advise friends to stay off the neighbor's new lawn.

_____ 10. Give generously to church and missions.

E.

Write yes or no to indicate whether you could PROTECT a neighbor's property in this way.

_____ 1. Tell a stranger that he left his car lights on.

_____ 2. Draw pictures in a library book.

_____ 3. Borrow school supplies and never return them.

_____ 4. Ride your bicycle across a soft lawn and make ruts.

_____ 5. Dissuade somebody from lying to the theater attendant about his or her age.

_____ 6. Write graffiti on the wall of a public building.

_____ 7. Tell a neighbor about a better way you have found for killing insects in the garden.

_____ 8. Accidentally break a window and neglect to admit your guilt.

_____ 9. Call the police if you see a thief breaking into a neighbor's home.

_____ 10. Sweep up the glass of a bottle you dropped on the street.

F.

Learn to spell these words. Use as many as you can in one sentence.

possessions   income   usury   fraud   steward

The Eighth Commandment

A.

Write these words or groups of words in the correct order to form a sentence.
The first word is italicized. Supply punctuation.

1. the Eighth Commandment   to safeguard reputation   *God* gave

_____

2. not give   your neighbor   false testimony   against   *You* shall

_____

3. part of the body   great boasts   is a small   *The* tongue   but it makes

_____

4. reputation   *A* shattered   be restored   cannot always

_____

5. a thief   is worse than   *A* slanderer

_____

B.

Underline the meaning which most closely fits the first word. Use a dictionary if necessary.

1. reputation: popularity—honor—dignity—good name
2. deceitfully: spitefully—wisely—hatefully—falsely
3. tell lies: pretend—misrepresent or withhold the truth—double-cross
4. betray: defraud—swindle—to be unfaithful to—falsify
5. slander: cheat—spread false reports—blame—dislike
6. defend: protect—forgive—respect—assist

C.

Draw a line from the name in the first column to the kind of false witness
which can be rendered in a courtroom.

1. Judge   knowingly presents falsified evidence
2. Witness   perverts or withholds the truth
3. Jury   renders an unjust verdict
4. Lawyer   accepts bribes

D.

Write the words tell lies, betray, slander, *or* hurt one's reputation *before the correct example.*

_____ 1. Syun loafed at home one Sunday morning and told his pastor that his father did not let him go to church.

_____ 2. Brett spread a rumor that he saw a church member drunk one night.

_____ 3. Laura wanted it to be kept secret that her father had been arrested for driving after having too much to drink. But a friend found out and told everyone in the neighborhood.

_____ 4. Andrea criticizes her teacher unfairly. As a result her parents think less and less of him.

E.

What would you do to follow the intent of the Commandment if

1. your big brother always complained about the choir? _____

   _____

2. your teacher scolded you undeservedly? _____

   _____

3. you were told that a local fruit stand had sold rotten strawberries? _____

   _____

4. you heard it said that a classmate had cheated? _____

   _____

5. you heard that the neighbors had a family quarrel?

   _____

6. you thought that your city mayor was being criticized unfairly? _____

   _____

7. your classmate wore clothes which you believed were too immodest? _____

   _____

8. you were with a group of people who were gossiping about a neighbor? _____

   _____

F.

Which commandment applies? Write the number of the Commandment on the blank line.

_____ 1. This commandment demands that you be pure in thought, word, and deed.

_____ 2. This commandment demands that you speak the truth at all times, especially to preserve your neighbor's good name.

_____ 3. This commandment demands that you do nothing to shorten or embitter a neighbor's life.

_____ 4. This commandment demands that you respect your neighbor's property and goods.

G.

Learn to spell these words. Use as many as you can in two sentences.

reputation   betray   slander

9
The Ninth and Tenth Commandments

A.

*Join the sentence beginnings of group 1 to the correct endings of group 2
by writing the key letters on the blank lines.*

Group 1

1. Covet means _____

2. It is a sin to wish to have those things _____

3. Both the Ninth and Tenth Commandments _____

4. The chief difference between these commandments is that one forbids the coveting of lifeless possessions while _____

5. These commandments require us to _____

Group 2

a. forbid us to covet our neighbor's blessings.

b. help our neighbor to keep his possessions.

c. "wish to have at the expense of others."

d. the other forbids the coveting of live possessions.

e. not intended for us or forbidden to us.

B.

Write out the commandment that corresponds to each number.

1. Regular church attendance _____

2. Obeying authority _____

3. Honesty _____

4. Chaste and decent sexuality _____

5. Truthfulness _____

6. Not using God's name in vain _____

7. Being content with what you have: _____

8. Helping a neighbor in time of need _____

9. Loving God above all things _____

C.

It is not sinful to "wish to have." But it is sinful to wish
to have AT THE EXPENSE OF SOMEONE ELSE! *Show how "wish" became "sinful covetousness" in each case of column 1 by writing its number in the correct space in column 2.*

Column 1

1. Paige wanted the highest grades in her class.
2. Jamal wanted a little more spending money.
3. Amy wanted a free afternoon to attend a show.
4. Brandon wished to use the family car, but his father said no.
5. Achan desired riches.
6. Kelsey wanted a leading role in the class play.
7. Cody wanted an ice-cream cone.
8. Jared wanted a dog.
9. Ahab wanted Naboth's vineyard.
10. Stephen's parents were on the lookout for an experienced child-care provider.

Column 2

_____ He killed Naboth to get it.

_____ He stole a parked car just to use for an evening.

_____ She slandered the girl chosen in her place.

_____ They hired one away from a family where the resources were limited and the mother was not well.

_____ He bought it with part of the money his parents gave him for church.

_____ She cheated on a test.

_____ He stole gold and silver.

_____ He coaxed a neighbor's dog to follow him home.

_____ He removed $5 from his father's wallet.

_____ She lied to her mother by saying she had to study at the library.

D.

Write a short definition for each of these expressions.

1. God is a jealous God. _____

2. God punishes sin. _____

E.

What commandment did each of these people disobey?

1. A murderer died in the electric chair. _____
2. A woman was imprisoned for lying in court. _____
3. A boy was punished for talking back to his teacher. _____
4. A woman lost her friends because of her envy. _____
5. A banker served a term in the penitentiary for embezzling money. _____
6. A man contracted a serious disease by leading an impure life. _____

F.

Learn to spell these words. Use as many as you can in two sentences.

covet   scheme   inheritance   entice   punishment   generations

⚏ **10** ⚏
The Law and Sin

A.

Write these words in the correct blank spaces of the paragraph.

line	whole	God	everyone	link
sin	breaking	Christ	no one	keep
perfectly	sufficient	Law	one	

Our holy God requires that we keep His Law_____. ___ _____ can do so
because _____ is a sinner. By nature, human beings think it is _____ merely to
do what is right. They are wrong. Even the best person cannot _____ God's _____ perfectly.
God says, "Whoever keeps the _____ law and yet stumbles at just _____
point is guilty of _____ all of it ." (James 2:10). Just as one crude _____ will spoil
a picture and one broken _____ will ruin a chain, so one little _____ makes us
unable to face _____ in our own righteousness. We are saved, not by our own works,
but through _____ who has kept the Law for us and died for our sins.

B.

The Law of God serves three purposes. These may be compared to three earthly objects.
Write the name of the object before the sentence it describes (curb, mirror, guide).

_____ 1. The Law shows you that your heart is stained by sin.
_____ 2. The Law is a signpost showing Christians what pleases God.
_____ 3. The Law checks the coarse outbursts of sin.

C.

Hymn 329 of Lutheran Worship *speaks of the purpose of God's Law.
Write the truths that appear in each stanza.*

Stanza 1. _____

_____

Stanza 2. _____

_____

Stanza 3. _____

_____

Stanza 4. _____

_____

D.

Follow the directions.

1. If it is a sin to miss God's target of perfection, circle the first letter. If not, circle the second.   I   H
2. If *iniquity* means "sneakiness," circle the first letter. If not, circle the second.   E   N
3. If sin is "lawlessness," circle the first letter. If not, circle the second.   E   S
4. If original sin is sin that we commit, circle the first letter. If not, circle the second.   A   E
5. If transgression means "un-equity," circle the first letter. If not, circle the second.   V   D
6. If it is sinful to turn from God's straight path, circle the first letter. If not, circle the second.   J   E
7. If sins earn eternal damnation, circle the first letter. If not, circle the second.   E   D
8. If Adam was the first to sin, circle the first letter. If not, circle the second.   M   S
9. If you sin only occasionally, circle the first letter. If you sin much every day, circle the second.   A   U
10. If death is the result of sin, circle the first letter. If not, circle the second.   S   N

E.

The sentences below tell briefly God's plan of salvation. Arrange them in the proper sequence by writing A, B, C, D, E, and F before them.

_____ Ever since Adam and Eve sinned, no mortal can keep God's Law perfectly.

_____ The devil was the first to sin.

_____ Now we are redeemed by Christ, and by His grace, through faith, we wear His righteousness like a white garment.

_____ The devil led Adam and Eve into sin.

_____ To be saved I must believe in Christ as my Savior from sin.

_____ The Lord Christ kept the Law perfectly in our stead and suffered the punishment of sin for us.

F.

Learn to spell the following words. Use as many as you can in three sentences.

transgression	wickedness	guile	actual	original
righteousness	omission	commission		

The Creed

A.

Write yes if the statement is true, and no if it is false.

_____ 1. A creed is a statement of what one believes.

_____ 2. The Apostles' Creed was written by Martin Luther.

_____ 3. *Believe* means only to "know with your mind."

_____ 4. "Creed" is from the Latin word *credo,* meaning "I believe."

_____ 5. One can be saved by another person's faith.

_____ 6. The devil knows that there is a God.

_____ 7. God the Father defends, guards, and protects only the believer.

_____ 8. God made all things with His hands.

_____ 9. In the sense of Creator, God is the Father of all human beings.

_____ 10. The only difference between humans and animals is that humans are far wiser.

_____ 11. It matters little what you believe, just so you believe.

_____ 12. *Create* here means, "Make something out of nothing."

_____ 13. "To believe" means "to trust."

B.

The three universal Christian creeds are the Apostles' Creed,
the Nicene Creed, and the Athanasian Creed.
They are found in *Lutheran Worship* on pages 142, 141, and 134–35 respectively.
Read them and write the name of the creed which applies to each of the descriptive phrases below.

_____ 1. sometimes called the "Twelve Articles."

_____ 2. named in honor of Athanasius.

_____ 3. written in Nicea.

_____ 4. is most commonly known.

_____ 5. explains most clearly that there are three divine Persons, yet only one Godhead.

_____ 6. particularly used on Trinity Sunday.

_____ 7. commonly used at Holy Communion and festival services.

_____ 8. contains essentially what the apostles believed.

_____ 9. most clearly states that Jesus is true God.

C.

Be prepared to read or recall a Bible passage text that shows each of the statements to be true. Write the Bible reference after each statement.

1. God made all visible and invisible creatures. _____

2. I must believe for myself if I am to be saved. _____

3. Since God created everyone, He is the Father of all. _____

4. To believe in God we must trust in Him. _____

5. God made heaven and earth out of nothing. _____

6. God is the true Father of Jesus. _____

7. The earth did not come of itself by evolution. _____

8. God is the Father of all believers in a special way. _____

D.

Learn to spell these words. Use as many as you can in three sentences.

Nicene   Athanasian   Creed   apostle   Creator   article

12

Angels, Human Beings and Preservation

A.

Write the first word (or words) of these sentence-endings.

1. _____ are the foremost among the invisible creatures.
2. _____ symbolize the rapid movement of angels.
3. _____ _____ show that angels are pure and holy.
4. _____ _____ serve God and Christians, especially children.
5. _____ _____ were all created holy.
6. _____ was even of high rank in heaven.
7. _____ _____ made themselves evil.
8. _____ can overcome the evil angels with the aid of Jesus, who is the Stronger than the strong.
9. _____ used the Word of God against Satan.

B.

Write three ways in which good and evil angels are alike.

1. _____
2. _____
3. _____

C.

In the first column write a word or phrase that describes the good angels.
In the second column write the opposite characteristic describing the evil angels.

Good	Evil
1. _____	1. _____
2. _____	2. _____
3. _____	3. _____

D.

If the sentence refers to the work of a good angel, write "Good" before it. If it refers to the work of an evil angel, write "Evil."

_____ 1. Andre has never had a bicycle accident.

_____ 2. Mercedes' family drove to and from church on an icy pavement without skidding.

_____ 3. Kumiko lied to the attendant about her age.

_____ 4. Thaddeus lost interest in the church shortly after confirmation.

_____ 5. Shaunda doubts the truth of creation because she read a book on evolution.

_____ 6. Joey's father has never been injured while working as an electrician.

E.

Place a check (✓) before those facts which show that human beings are the foremost among the visible creatures.

_____ 1. We have a brain.

_____ 2. We have an immortal soul.

_____ 3. We rule the earth as God's representatives.

_____ 4. We die.

_____ 5. We were created.

_____ 6. We can solve problems through reasoning.

_____ 7. We are made in God's image.

_____ 8. We can learn.

_____ 9. We stand erect.

_____ 10. We can speak.

F.

Underline the ending that is most correct.

1. The "divine image" means chiefly that humans were created
   intelligent   able to speak   without sin.

2. We no longer have the "divine image" because
   our mind is beclouded   Adam and Eve sinned   we are wicked.

3. The "divine image" is partly renewed in
   believers   church members   little children.

4. The "divine image" will be restored fully when we
   enter heaven   believe   live right.

G.

Tell how God preserves and defends you as to

1. clothing _____

2. food _____

3. drink _____

4. health _____

5. shelter _____

6. happiness _____

H.

Learn to spell the following words. Use as many as you can in two sentences.

immortal   divine   creation   Satan   worthiness

⧟ 13 ⧟
The Second Article

A.

Fill in the missing parts.

1. Jesus means _____.

2. [The angel said to Joseph,] "Do _____ to take
   _____, because _____ is from
   _____. She will give birth to a son, and
   _____, because He will
   _____." (Matthew 1:20–21)

3. Christ means the _____One. The Hebrew word is _____.

4. "Christ" is not a name, but a _____, as _____ or _____.

5. Christ was anointed to be our _____, _____, and _____.

B.

The Holy Scriptures give numerous other names to Jesus Christ.
Look up these references below and write the names on the lines.

John 20:28 _____ and _____.

Jeremiah 23:6 _____ our _____.

John 1:14 _____.

Matthew 9:6 _____ of _____.

Isaiah 9:6 _____ _____, _____ _____,
_____ _____, _____ of _____.

Acts 3:15 _____ of _____.

C.

Poets have given numerous other names to Jesus. *Look up these hymns in* Lutheran Worship
and write the names by which He is called.

Hymn 48, Stanza 3: _____   _____

Hymn 18, Stanza 3: _____

Hymn 31, Stanza 1: _____

Hymn 176, Stanza 1: _____

Hymn 264, Stanza 1: _____, _____

Hymn 114, Stanza 1: _____ of _____

D.

Copy the words from Luther's Explanation of the Second Article which tell that

1. Jesus is fully divine.

_____

_____

2. Jesus is fully human.

_____

_____

E.

Underline those words or phrases which show Christ's divine nature.

1. suffered
2. hungry
3. tempted by Satan
4. adored by angels
5. unchangeable
6. walked on the sea

7. holy
8. omniscient
9. was crucified
10. performed miracles
11. rose from the dead
12. born in a manger

13. almighty
14. I AM
15. shall judge
16. wept
17. slept
18. healed those with leprosy

F.

Underline those words or phrases which describe Christ's human nature.

1. born of a woman
2. grew tired
3. ascended to heaven
4. worked
5. died
6. ate and drank

7. was crucified
8. walked with His disciples
9. drove out devils
10. all-present
11. suffered
12. kept the Law perfectly

13. raised Lazarus
14. spoke to His disciples
15. wept
16. prayed
17. healed the sick
18. was tempted

G.

If only God could do so, write "God" before the word or phrase. If man could do so, write "Man."

_____ 1. be under the Ten Commandments

_____ 2. overcome sin, death, and the devil

_____ 3. keep the Law without sinning once

_____ 4. suffer and die

_____ 5. raise Himself from the dead

H.

Learn to spell these words. Try to use all of them in three sentences.

Jesus Christ   Messiah   anointed   eternity   conceived   Pontius Pilate

14
The Second Article
(Christ's Humiliation)

A.

Join the sentence halves by writing on the lines the key letters of the endings.

1. As our Priest, Christ sacrificed _____

2. As a prophet, Christ preached _____

3. Christ is a king who rules over _____

4. As our Prophet, Christ now preaches

   _____

5. Christ pleads for us even as the

   _____

6. The threefold kingdom of Christ is the

   _____

7. As our Priest, Christ fulfilled _____

8. A miter and scepter symbolize _____

a. everything, especially over the Christian church.

b. priests of the Old Testament pleaded to God for the people.

c. the Law perfectly for us.

d. to the people in and around Judea and Galilee.

e. Kingdom of Power, Grace, and Glory.

f. Christ as our King.

g. Himself as the Lamb of God upon the altar of the cross.

h. through His ministers.

B.

Each of the Bible references below speaks of one of the six steps of Christ's state of humiliation. Look up each reference, write the appropriate word from the following list:

conceived,   born,   suffered,   crucified,   died,   buried.

Matthew 27:59–60 _____

Luke 1:35 _____

Mark 15:37 _____

Luke 2:11 _____

John 19:18 _____

John 19:1–2 _____

C.

Read this story and circle the best of the titles found below.

God made the first pair of human beings. He made them both holy. He placed them into the Garden of Happiness. He loved them as His own dear children and desired that they should always be with Him.

For reasons all His own God did not make them blind slaves to His will, as were the sun, moon, and stars, but He gave them freedom of will, the right to choose between good and evil.

When the time came to choose, Satan—a fallen angel—was on hand to offer advice, with the result that the man and woman decided to choose their will over God's will. The creature disobeyed the Creator, and thus sin entered into the world, and death by sin.

But God still loved His human creatures. And He revealed to them His plan to restore His creation. He told them of the "Woman's Seed" (Jesus, the virgin-born) who will bruise the head of the serpent (Satan).

"But when the time had fully come, God sent His Son, born of a woman, born under law, to redeem those under law, that we might receive the full rights of sons" (Galatians 4:4–5).

Paradise lost! Paradise regained? Yes, through Jesus Christ, the Son of God, the Son of Man.

Titles: Adam and Eve in the Garden
Satan's Power of Persuasion
Redemption for Fallen Humankind
How Humans Became Sinful

D.

Join the FACTS to the correct REASONS, taking for granted that in each case the person is a true believer in Christ.

Fact

_____ 1. The criminal knew that his sins would not bar him from heaven.

_____ 2. Eric overcame a temptation to look at indecent pictures.

_____ 3. The wounded soldier was not afraid to die.

_____ 4. Ana was greatly distressed because of a sin she had committed. But after she had confessed it to Jesus and asked for pardon, she felt free and happy.

_____ 5. Since becoming a believer, Minh no longer fears the power of Satan.

_____ 6. Lazarus died and the angels carried his soul to heaven.

Reason

1. Jesus gave him power to resist the temptation.

2. Jesus redeemed her from the guilt of sin.

3. Jesus saved him from the second death.

4. Jesus, who had saved the malefactor on the cross, would save also him.

5. Jesus had robbed death of its sting.

6. Jesus redeemed him from the ownership of Satan.

E.

The greatest sacrifice a person can make is to give up his
or her life for another. Christ gave His life for us.
*Below are a number of ways in which we can show our thankfulness
to Christ for His boundless love.*
Place a (✓) in the column to express your interest or participation in serving Christ.

	I would like to serve	I am serving now	I hope to serve someday
1. Hear His Word in church and Bible class every Sunday.			
2. Speak up for Christ when someone ridicules the church.			
3. Give a proportionate part of your money to church and missions.			
4. Avoid profanity and misuse of God's name.			
5. Avoid unclean thoughts.			
6. Give up some free time to help your pastor or teacher.			
7. Consider becoming a pastor or teacher.			
8. Teach Sunday school.			
9. Help in your congregation's evangelism ministry.			
10. Become a missionary.			

F.

Learn to spell these words. Use as many as you can in two sentences.

humiliation   exaltation   prophet   crucified   Redeemer

≈ 15 ≈
The Second Article
(Christ's Exaltation)

A. Descended

Circle the Y (yes) before the true statements and the N (no) before the false statements.

Y N 1. Jesus descended into hell some time after He had awakened on Easter morning and before He appeared to His disciples.

Y N 2. The Lord descended into hell to show Himself to the devil as the Victor.

Y N 3. "Descended into hell" means "Was placed into the grave."

Y N 4. Believers who died before Christ's coming could not go to heaven immediately but had to stay in "Limbo" until Christ released them.

Y N 5. Jesus descended into hell to suffer its torments for us.

Y N 6. Those who die in unbelief are forever lost without being given a "second chance" by Christ.

Y N 7. We may be unafraid of Satan and hell because Christ proved by His descent that He has conquered them.

B. Rose

1. After the resurrection, Christ had the same body, yet it was different. *Write "S" if the statement shows Christ's body was the Same, and "D" if it shows that His body was Different.*

_____ a. He ate with His disciples.

_____ b. At first Mary thought Him to be the gardener.

_____ c. He no longer felt the pain of His wounds.

_____ d. His disciples touched Him.

_____ e. He rose without disturbing the grave linens.

_____ f. He entered a locked room.

_____ g. He talked with His disciples.

_____ h. He disappeared at Emmaus.

_____ i. He ascended into heaven.

_____ j. Seven disciples by the sea did not recognize Him.

2. *In three short sentences give reasons why we can be certain that Christ rose bodily from the dead.*

a. _____

b. _____

c. _____

3. Recall a Bible passage that shows each of these statements to be true. Write the Bible reference on the blank line.

    a. Christ's resurrection proves Him to be God's Son._____

    b. The resurrection proves that God was satisfied with His Son's suffering
       for sin._____

    c. All believers shall rise to eternal life._____

C. Ascended

The two chief accounts of our Lord's ascension are found in Luke 24:50–53 and Acts 1:1–11. Although both accounts were written by St. Luke, they are not identical. *Read them and indicate whether these events were recorded in Luke's Gospel or in the Acts by writing L (Luke) or A (Acts) before them. In some cases you may use both letters.*

_____ 1. Jesus led them out to Bethany.

_____ 2. This occurred 40 days after Easter.

_____ 3. Jesus commanded that after the Ascension the disciples should wait in Jerusalem for the coming of the Holy Spirit.

_____ 4. Jesus raised His hands to bless them.

_____ 5. Jesus ascended until a cloud hid Him from their view.

_____ 6. Jesus rose into heaven.

_____ 7. Two angels appeared and told the disciples He would come again.

_____ 8. The Ascension was from the Mount of Olives.

_____ 9. The disciples returned to Jerusalem with great joy.

D.

Read Ephesians 1:18–23. Write the words of this Bible passage that refer to Christ's ascension.

_____

_____

_____

_____

E.

1. *Read Matthew 24:1–51. List signs of the approach of the Last Day.*

    1. _____.

    2. _____.

    3. _____.

    4. _____.

    5. _____.

2. *Write these words into the correct blank spaces of the paragraph.*

believers	Come	angels	Depart	innocence
heaven	righteousness	blessedness	served	unbelievers
Jesus	nations	living	see	judged
dead	kingdom	Last Day	fear	soon
own				

Our ascended Lord will come again on the _____ _____, with all His holy _____, to judge the _____ and the _____. The _____ will try to flee from Him when they _____ Him come, but the _____ will be happy because they will know that He is coming to take them to _____. The graves will open and the dead of all _____ will come forth to stand before the throne of _____ to be _____. To the believers who _____ Him Jesus will say, "_____, you who are blessed by My Father; take your inheritance, the kingdom prepared for you since the creation of the world" (Matthew 25:34). To the unbelievers He will say, "_____ from Me, you who are cursed, into the eternal fire" (Matthew 25:41).

I will not _____ the coming of Christ. Instead I will pray that He returns _____ to take me home. I am His _____ and want to live under Him in His _____ and serve Him in everlasting _____, _____, and _____.

F.

Learn to spell these words. Use as many as you can in two sentences.

resurrection	righteousness	descended
ascended	innocence	blessedness

16
The Third Article
(Sanctification)

A.

*Write these words and phrases in the correct sequence to form sentences.
The first word of each sentence is italicized. Supply punctuation.*

1. in the Holy Trinity   is the   Third Person   *The* Holy Spirit

2. Spirit   is true   *The* Holy   God

3. by inspiration   *The* Bible   of the Holy Spirit   was written

4. is the   to Jesus   Holy Spirit   *My* Guide

5. the Word of God   *The* Holy Spirit   through   makes Christians of us

6. were made   were baptized   *Most* of us   Christians   when we

B.

Join the words to the correct explanatory definitions by drawing lines from dash to dash.

1. Spiritually blind —

   Spiritually dead —

   Enemy of God —

2. Called me —

   Enlightened me —

   Sanctified me —

   Kept me —

— "Eat, drink, and be merry" is my philosophy.

— Saul (Paul) hated Jesus and those who believed in Him.

— "I don't see why God should punish an innocent person like Jesus. I don't want a scapegoat for my sins."

— does not let me stray from the love of Jesus.

— teaches me to be sure of my salvation in Christ.

— invites me to trust Christ as Savior and works faith in my heart.

— gives me power to resist sin, to lead a Christian life, and to do good works.

C.

*Draw a small (+) before the acts which are signs of a sanctified life.
Leave the lines blank before those which are not good works.*

_____ 1. Say a silent prayer upon entering church.

_____ 2. Pray for someone who hates you.

_____ 3. Annoy your teacher with mischievous behavior.

_____ 4. Hold your temper.

_____ 5. Go to church only when your parents remind you to do so.

_____ 6. Cut the grass for an elderly neighbor.

_____ 7. Tell the clerk when she has given you too much change.

_____ 8. Listen to God speak through His Word.

_____ 9. Take part in fights frequently.

_____ 10. Admit your guilt if you have done wrong.

_____ 11. Grumble because your parents can't afford to increase your weekly allowance.

_____ 12. Help your parents cheerfully whenever asked.

D.

Circle as many endings as are correct. One, two, or all three may be correct.

1. At birth I was spiritually
   a. not quite perfect;
   b. too young to be sinful;
   c. blind, dead, and an enemy of God.

2. When an unbeliever is converted he or she
   a. becomes a believer;
   b. begins to serve Christ;
   c. strays farther from God.

3. The Holy Spirit desires to work faith in everyone who hears the Gospel, but many people
   a. resist Him;
   b. are too sinful to become believers;
   c. never hear the Gospel.

4. When a person is saved, the glory belongs to
   a. the pastor who preached the Gospel;
   b. the congregation that pays the pastor;
   c. the Holy Spirit.

5. The Third Person of the Trinity is called the *Holy* Spirit because
   a. He calls through God's holy Word;
   b. He Himself is holy;
   c. He makes us holy.

6. People who have been made holy by the Holy Spirit are called
   a. Christians;
   b. Gentiles;
   c. believers.

7. A Christian is one who
   a. believes in Jesus;
   b. Loves Jesus;
   c. follows Jesus.

8. Christians do good works because
   a. they must do their part in earning a place in heaven;
   b. by doing so they can keep themselves in the faith;
   c. faith is a living faith that serves in love.

E.

We can daily thank the Holy Spirit for having brought us to faith in Jesus.
Tell the story of your Christian biography by writing answers to the questionnaire below.

1. At what occasion did the Holy Spirit call you? At my

_____

_____

_____

_____

2. In which ways were you enlightened by the Holy Spirit since being called? (In home, school, church, etc.)

_____

_____

_____

_____

3. What means does the Holy Spirit use to keep you in the true faith until your dying day? (In school, church, home, etc.)

_____

_____

_____

_____

F.

Learn to spell these words. Use as many as you can in two sentences.

sanctified   conversion   Christian   enlightened   spiritually

The Holy Christian Church

A. The Invisible Church

1. The word in italics in each sentence is WRONG. Draw a line through that word and write the correct word on the blank line.

   a. The whole company of believers in heaven and on earth is known as the *visible* church. _____

   b. The Holy Spirit calls people and makes them Christians through the preaching of the *Law*. _____

   c. The true church of God is known on earth as the Kingdom of *Glory*.
   _____

   d. Another name for the Kingdom of Glory is the Church *Militant*.
   _____

   e. We *can* look into another person's heart to see whether he has faith. _____

   f. Only the *pastor* knows who are the true members of the holy Christian church. _____

   g. We say "holy Christian church" because her members all believe in *holiness*.
   _____

   h. Although believers still sin daily, yet by reason of their faith in Christ they are *imperfect* in God's sight. _____

2. From the Third Article copy those words which mean the same as "The holy Christian church."

   _____

   _____

   _____

B. The Visible Church

1. Write the name of five church *denominations*.

   _____

   _____

   _____

   _____

   _____

2. Write the name of your denomination.

   _____

3. Write the names and locations of three other *congregations* of your denomination.

Name   Location

_____   _____

_____   _____

_____   _____

4. How many *"souls"* or baptized members are there in your congregation?

_____

How many *confirmed members?* _____

Why can we not be certain that all of them belong to the invisible church?

_____

What word describes those who, though belonging to a visible church, are not true believers? _____

C.

The true visible church is the one that bases all teachings on the Word of God—the Bible. Any church that teaches a doctrine not found in the Bible cannot be the true visible church. *Below are listed several false teachings. Using the Word of God, prove these doctrines to be false. Write the first five or six words of a Bible passage you would use in each case.*

1. Jesus was the greatest teacher who ever lived, but He was not God.

_____

_____

_____

2. All people are by nature very good, sometimes without sin.

_____

_____

_____

3. It does not matter what you believe, only that you believe something.

_____

_____

_____

4. In the end, all people will go to heaven, regardless of their religion.

_____

_____

_____

D.

Circle the names of those who show that they believe and live the doctrine of the church.

1. Jesse, a confirmed member of a Lutheran church, attended rather regularly, but didn't have faith in Jesus.
2. Danetta sincerely professed her faith at her confirmation and prayed that she might be an active member of the congregation.
3. Lorenzo was confirmed in the Lutheran church, but he says it doesn't matter what church a person attends.
4. Mr. Williams served as church treasurer for 18 years because he wished to serve Christ and His people.
5. Mrs. Schmidt volunteers at the church office every week to help prepare the Sunday bulletin.
6. Joel says he's a true believer but doesn't care to join a church because, he says, there are "too many hypocrites."
7. Thomas gives little towards missions because he believes that "charity begins at home."
8. The Jones family moved to a different city and affiliated with the Lutheran church in that town as soon as possible.
9. Amanda went to her pastor to learn the difference between her church's teachings and her best friend's church. Just last week her friend said, "Come to my church. It's practically the same as yours."
10. Terrance regards it as a privilege to serve his Lord by teaching vacation Bible school.
11. Mark spent his summers with his grandparents on a farm. He got permission from his pastor to receive Holy Communion in the church where his grandparents were members.

E.

Learn to spell these words. Use as many as you can in three sentences.

Catholic	Protestant	Lutheran	militant
triumphant	Reformation	evangelical	

The Forgiveness of Sins (Justification)
The Resurrection of the Body
Life Everlasting

A. The Forgiveness of Sins

1. *Fill in the missing words.*

   a. _____ grants forgiveness of sins daily and richly to _____ and all _____ .

   b. God forgives my sins for _____ sake.

   c. Jesus lived, _____, and _____ again for me.

   d. Jesus gained forgiveness for all _____.

   e. God bestows His forgiveness through the _____ and the two _____.

   f. On the _____ _____, God will raise _____ and all _____ _____.

   g. God will give _____ _____ to me and _____ _____.

   h. The central teaching of the Gospel is this that all who believe receive _____ of _____ and are _____ before God, not by _____ , but by _____, for Jesus' sake, through _____.

2. *Arrange the thoughts into a sequence that best tells the story of justification by grace, through faith, for Christ's sake.*

   ___ Jesus took on Himself the guilt of my sin and suffered the punishment in my stead.

   ___ I received the forgiveness Jesus earned by believing that God has declared me justified for Jesus' sake.

   ___ My heart was by nature dead to God, black from the evil of sin. In this condition I could not stand before my God, for I deserved nothing but punishment.

   ___ The blood that Jesus shed washed the guilt from my heart and made it clean and holy in God's sight.

B. The Resurrection of the Body

1. *Draw a line from the Bible reference to the name of the person whose body was raised from the dead.*

   John 11:41–46   Dorcas

   1 Kings 17:17–24   The Widow's Son

   Acts 9:36–42   The Daughter of Jairus

   Mark 5:35–43   Jesus

   Luke 7:11–18   Lazarus

   Matthew 28:5–7   Eutychus

   Matthew 27:50–53   The Man in Elisha's Sepulcher

   Acts 20:7–12   The Young Man of Nain

   2 Kings 13:20–21   Saints

2. *Copy the words of the Third Article of the Nicene Creed which refer to the resurrection of the body.*

   _____

   _____

C. Life Everlasting

Thought questions. Formulate a brief answer to each of these questions and be prepared to tell your answer in your own words.

1. Why are people sad at funerals?
2. Is it wrong to cry at the funeral of a believer? State the reason for your answer.
3. Why may a funeral service for a Christian be called "A Celebration of Victory"?
4. In what respects is death like sleep?
5. Why do you not need to be afraid to die?
6. What is the best way to prepare for a blessed death?
7. When will both your soul and body be able to rejoice with God and the saints in heaven?
8. If a believer's death is blessed, why does God allow many believers to remain on earth to old age?

D.

In the boxes labeled Heaven, Earth, and Hell write the numbers of the statements which describe life in those places. Some numbers may be used in two boxes.

1. Sickness
2. Disobedience
3. See God "face to face"
4. Torments
5. No more sin
6. Perfect health
7. Gnashing of teeth
8. Enmity
9. Worry
10. Bodily death
11. Hard work
12. No weeping
13. Complete separation from God
14. Hunger and thirst
15. Marriage
16. Eternal life
17. Cursing
18. Spiritual death
19. Perfect renewal of the divine image
20. Church militant
21. Church triumphant
22. Praise God
23. Eternal death
24. Hatred

Heaven

Earth

Hell

E.

Cross out those activities that do not help you to prepare for a blessed death.

1. Trying to read the future through tarot cards
2. Attending Bible class
3. Giving little for missions
4. Sincere daily praying
5. Receiving the Lord's Supper frequently
6. Indecent speech
7. Envy
8. Forgiving those who trespass against you
9. Giving to the needy
10. Telling unbelievers of Jesus' love
11. Being truly sorry for one's sins
12. Sleeping during the sermon
13. Studying God's Word
14. Watching indecent movies
15. Unwilling to take part in church work
16. Remembering Jesus' dying love
17. Not concerned about your relationship with God

F.

Learn to spell these words. Try to use them in two sentences.

forgiveness   justified   everlasting   heaven

19
Prayer

A.

Follow the directions.

1. If praying is "talking with God," circle H. If not, circle S.   H   S

2. If God hears every prayer, circle the E. If not, circle P.   E   P

3. If we may pray only to ask God for blessings, circle E.
   If we may also pray to give thanks, circle W.   E   W

4. If Revelation 19:10 tells us to worship angels, circle A. If not, circle I.   A   I

5. If saints in heaven hear our prayers and offer their prayers to God for us,
   circle K. If not, circle L.   K   L

6. If Christians rightly add, "If You are willing" to prayers for earthly
   blessings, circle L. If not, circle T.   L   T

7. If praying in Jesus' name is only a fine custom, circle O. If Jesus
   commanded and invited us to pray in that manner, circle G.   O   G

8. If a mother may rightly pray for her dead son, circle G. If it is useless
   for her to do so, circle I.   G   I

9. If "Pray without ceasing" means, "Pray at all times," circle V. If not,
   circle O.   O   V

10. If you may rightly pray for someone who hates you, circle E.
    If not, circle D.   E   D

11. If bowing your head and kneeling are outward signs of humility
    before God, circle I. If not, circle D.   I   D

12. If a devout believer can get along without praying, circle A.
    If he needs prayer, circle T.   A   T

13. If grown people need bedtime prayer as much as little children, circle Y.
    If not, circle I.   Y   I

14. If thoughtless or mechanical praying helps, circle L. If such praying
    is useless, circle O.   L   O

15. If praying should be done only in time of trouble, circle Y. If praying
    should be done at all times, circle U.   Y   U

B.

What is unhealthy in the prayer life of these people?

1. Matthew prays only when others are praying with him, e. g., in church or in the family circle.

   _____

   _____

2. Elena doesn't think of what the pastor is saying when he prays before the altar.

   _____

   _____

3. If mother forgets to remind her, Danielle goes to bed without praying.

   _____

   _____

4. Since becoming a high school student, Jordan thinks bedtime prayers are only for children.

   _____

   _____

5. A very wealthy man didn't pray because he had all the material blessings he wanted.

   _____

   _____

6. A father prayed fervently for his sick wife, but she died. Now he says, "What good does it do to pray?"

   _____

   _____

7. Kenneth prays only for himself and his family.

   _____

   _____

8. Jennifer prays only those prayers which she has memorized.

   _____

   _____

C.

Join the sentence endings of group 2 to the sentence beginnings of group 1 by writing the key letters on the blank lines.

Group 1

1. Prayer is to the soul what _____
2. When praying becomes unpleasant or irksome, _____
3. We should pray only to the triune God because _____
4. God answers our prayer even if we ask for something _____
5. Because Jesus is the Way into the presence of God _____
6. A Christian will want to pray at least _____
7. Three good places for prayer are _____
8. Folding your hands and bowing your head _____
9. The Lord's Prayer is _____

Group 2

a. all prayers should be made in His name.
b. He alone can and will hear us.
c. church, school, and home.
d. the model prayer, because it asks for the best things in the best way.
e. breath is to the body.
f. every morning and evening, before and after meals.
g. help to keep your hands and eyes from distraction.
h. the soul is sick.
i. which He knows will harm us, but He answers it by saying no.

D. Special Exercises

1. Write a short birthday prayer in which you thank God for having blessed you during another year.

   _____
   _____
   _____

2. List six physical blessings for which you could pray.

   _____ _____ _____
   _____ _____ _____

3. List four spiritual blessings for which you could pray.

   _____ _____
   _____ _____

4. List six people whom you might include in your prayers. Have you ever done so?

   _____ _____ _____
   _____ _____ _____

E.

Learn to spell these words. Use each one in a sentence.

petition   meditation   intercession

20
The Lord's Prayer

A. The Introduction

Use these words to fill in the blank spaces

believer	loves	help	selfish	unbeliever
troubles	hear	Our	grant	hesitate
neighbor	Father	Lord		

1. _____ Father who art in heaven.

2. When I say "Our" I am also praying for my _____.

3. My neighbor is any person who needs my prayers, a _____ as well as an _____.

4. My praying would be _____ if I prayed only for myself.

5. Jesus wants me to address God as _____ because He _____ me.

6. I need never _____ to come to my heavenly Father to tell Him my _____, for I know He is always willing to _____ me.

7. "Who art in heaven" should remind me that the heavenly Father is the _____ over all, who can both _____ and _____ my requests.

B. The First Petition

Draw a line through the three sentences that have no direct connection with the First Petition.

1. God's name is as holy as God is.
2. Lord, enable my pastor to preach Your Word with power.
3. God's names tell us briefly who He is.
4. Lord, may Your Word be kept holy.
5. All good gifts come from God.
6. Teaching false doctrine profanes God's name.
7. God will forgive any repentant believer.
8. A God-pleasing life serves to hallow God's name.
9. Lord, protect my body from danger.
10. Lord, grant that I may live according to Your Word.

C. The Second Petition

This petition is a great missionary prayer. *Circle the names of those who show that they want the Christian church to grow.*

1. Miguel prayed that God would give courage and health to missionaries at home and abroad.
2. Larissa encourages a friend to attend the Christian day school.
3. Keith frequently tells his unchurched pal the story of the movie he saw, but he never tells him the Bible story he learned in school.
4. Lora seldom gives for missions.
5. Zachary persuaded a high school friend to take instruction for confirmation.
6. While on a flight Byron told a fellow passenger of the joy he derives from serving the church.
7. Paul won't wear a miniature cross on his shirt because he fears that his friends will tease him about being a "Sunday school guy."

D. The Third Petition

Write these words, phrases, and clauses as sentences.
The first word of each sentence is italicized. Supply punctuation.

1. obey God's will   in heaven   *The* angels   perfectly

_____

_____

2. on earth the world   oppose God's will   *The* devil and our flesh

_____

_____

3. that all people believe   in Jesus   *God's* will is   and love one another

_____

_____

4. to do His will   we ask God   of the unholy three   *In* this petition   and lead us
to break the will

_____

_____

_____

E. The Fourth Petition

Underline the correct words.

1. God gives earthly blessings without our asking, even to all the—*believers, sinners, wicked.*
2. God would have us thank Him every—*day, week, year*—for earthly blessings.
3. By the Spirit's power we share our blessings with—*important, poor, friendly*—people.
4. God would not have us—*think about, plan for, worry about*—the future.
5. This petition asks God for all the earthly blessing we—*need, want, covet.*
6. We may pray for—*earthly, spiritual*—blessings.

F. The Fifth Petition

Read the story of the unforgiving servant in Matthew 18:23–35. Match the various parts of the story with the similar meanings in the second column.

1. The King
2. The servant who owed 10,000 talents
3. The debt of 10,000 talents
4. The fellow servant
5. The debt of 100 denarii

___Sins committed against God.

___Sins against others

___A person who sinned against another person

___Our heavenly Father

___A person who sinned against God

Underline the Bible passage that best summarizes the "lesson point" of the parable of the unmerciful servant.

1. "Come to me, all you who are weary and burdened, and I will give you rest." (Matthew 11:28)

2. "If we confess our sins, He is faithful and just and will forgive us our sins and purify us from all unrighteousness." (1 John 1:9)

3. "For if you forgive men when they sin against you, your heavenly Father will also forgive you. But if you do not forgive men their sins, your Father will not forgive your sins." (Matthew 6:14–15)

G. The Sixth Petition

Match the facts with the reasons.

Facts

1. God permits troubles to enter the lives of believers. _____
2. God never tempts us to sin. _____
3. We ask God to protect us from the devil's temptations. _____
4. Adversity may be helpful in a believer's life. _____

Reasons

1. God is holy.
2. We cannot resist the devil with our might alone.
3. God strengthens our faith during times of trouble and makes us more patient.
4. God wishes to test their faith to make it stronger.

H. The Seventh Petition

1. Think of three evils that could come to your body, soul, and family.

_____
_____
_____

2. What is the worst evil that could befall your soul and body?

_____
_____

3. Write a one-sentence prayer asking God to grant you a blessed death.

_____
_____
_____

I. The Conclusion

Match the phrases of column 1 to the explanations of column 2 by writing the key numbers on the blank lines. Then look up these passages in your Bible and write them behind the correct explanation in column 3. John 16:23. Psalm 24:1. Psalm 145:21. Philippians 4:19.

Column 1

1. For Thine is the kingdom.

2. Thine is the power.

3. Thine is the glory.

4. Amen.

Column 2

_____ All honor belongs to You, O Lord.

_____ It shall be so.

_____ All authority and majesty belong to You.

_____ All things belong to You.

Column 3

_____

_____

_____

_____

J.

Learn to spell these words. Use as many as you can in three sentences.

hallowed   missionary   trespass   temptation   pious

The Nature of Baptism

A.

Make sentences by crossing out the words you do not need.

1. A sacrament is a (worldly—sacred) act (ordained—permitted) by God. By certain (visible—invisible) means and His (love—Word) God gives us (peace—forgiveness).
2. There are (seven—two—many) sacraments.
3. The rite of marriage is not a sacrament because (God's Word—forgiveness) is lacking.
4. The visible means in (the Lord's Supper—Baptism) is (water—God's Word—a sponsor).
5. Bread and wine are the visible (sacramentals—means) in (Baptism—the Lord's Supper).

B.

Circle the Y (yes) before true statements and the N (no) before false statements.

Y N   1. Holy Baptism was ordained by John the Baptist.
Y N   2. A Baptism is valid only if it is performed by a pastor.
Y N   3. "Make disciples" means to make believers, followers.
Y N   4. Baptism's power to forgive sins lies in the water.
Y N   5. "All nations" means all people—babies, small children, and adults.
Y N   6. Baptism by immersing is valid in God's sight.
Y N   7. The power of the Holy Trinity is present in Baptism.
Y N   8. In general, other liquids may be used instead of water for baptizing.
Y N   9. Only adults can believe.
Y N 10. A Baptism is valid without the child's actual sponsors being present.
Y N 11. Baptism is a ceremony for giving a child a name.

C.

List three reasons why children should be baptized.

1. _____

_____

2. _____

_____

3. _____

_____

D.

Draw a line through descriptions of people who ought NOT to be chosen as sponsors at a Baptism.

1. A devout believing adult
2. A person of a different religion
3. A young child who has not yet been confirmed
4. A friendly neighbor who has no church affiliation
5. The parents of the child to be baptized
6. A believing relative who lives in a distant city
7. A non-Christian family acquaintance
8. A person who doubts the power of Baptism
9. A close friend who belongs to no church

E.

List four ways in which water can be applied in Baptism.

1. _____
2. _____
3. _____
4. _____

F.

Using your baptismal certificate, answer these questions.

1. Who baptized you? _____ When? _____
2. Where? _____ Place? _____
   (City—County—State)   (Home—Church)
3. Name of congregation? _____
4. Who were your sponsors? _____
   _____

G.

1. Although a Baptism in the home is just as valid in God's sight as one performed in church, why does the church, under normal circumstances, baptize at the church?

2. Have you ever witnessed a Baptism in a home or church? If not, perhaps your pastor will make arrangements for you to witness one soon, so that you can *answer these questions regarding the ceremony.*

   a. Why did the pastor refer to the story of Jesus' blessing little children?

   _____

   b. Who spoke for the child? _____

   c. Write two or more responsibilities of parents and sponsors.

   1) _____
   2) _____
   3) _____

   d. Write the words the pastor spoke while baptizing.

   _____
   _____

3. Why are sponsors not used when an adult is baptized?

   _____

H.

Learn to spell these words. Use as many as you can in three sentences.

Sacrament   Baptism   baptize   ordained   sponsor

22
Blessings, Power, and Significance of Baptism

A. The Blessings of Baptism

If the two or three sentences lead to a correct conclusion, write "Correct" on the blank line.
If they lead to an incorrect conclusion, write "Incorrect."

1. A little baby has original sin.
   Sin separates from God.
   Baptism works forgiveness of sins.
   Therefore, a little baby needs Baptism to come to God.

   _____

2. The devil is always eager to make people sin.
   Sinful humans cannot by their own strength fight the devil.
   Baptism gives deliverance from the devil.
   Therefore, baptized people need no longer worry about being tempted by the devil.

   _____

3. Spiritual death may end in eternal damnation.
   Baptism delivers from spiritual death.
   Therefore, once baptized, a person can no longer be damned.

   _____

4. Whoever believes and is baptized will be saved.
   Whoever does not believe will be condemned.
   Therefore, it is really unbelief that condemns.

   _____

5. Unbelief condemns.
   Faith saves.
   A person who has faith in Jesus can be saved without Baptism
   (e.g., the thief on the cross).
   Therefore, Baptism isn't very important for our salvation.

   _____

B. The Power of Baptism

Fill in what you think would be the final rhyming word of each couplet.

1. When I was but an infant small,
   My parents heard the Savior

   _____,

2. "Let your child come to Me
   That he or she My grace may

   _____."

3. They gladly heard His promise true
   And brought me to a life brand

   _____.

4. The human mind can't understand
   How, when the pastor dipped his

   _____,

5. The water flowed upon my head
   As God's baptismal Word was

   _____,

6. That washing took my sins away
   And placed me on the heavenly

   _____

7. Which leads to Jesus' loving arm,
   Where I am free from Satan's

   _____.

8. The water does no mighty things,
   God's Word of life rich blessing

   _____.

9. His Gospel grace alone can give
   The water power to make souls

   _____.

10. From Word and water I receive
    God's saving grace, as I

    _____.

C. The Significance of Baptizing with Water

Match the words with the definitions by writing the numbers before the words.
One definition is used twice.

Words

___ signifies
___ Old Adam
___ contrition
___ repentance
___ be drowned
___ new man
___ righteousness
___ purity
___ chapter six
___ buried with Christ
___ newness of life

Definitions

1. heart-sorrow, regret over sin
2. uprightness, holiness
3. be overcome
4. our sinful nature is put to death
5. means, makes known
6. cleaned from sin
7. our sinful nature
8. a life of God-pleasing deeds
9. sorrow for sin, faith in Christ, and the intention to better one's life
10. Romans passage

D.

Circle the names of those baptized people whose life shows that they walk in "newness of life."

1. Keeven prays for forgiveness every night.
2. Dawn causes her parents untold worry through her disobedience.
3. Karl associates continually with a group of boys who have a bad reputation in the community.
4. Brad is always willing to serve the church on special committees.
5. Kimberly is known for her honesty and truthfulness.
6. Gerald receives the Lord's Supper regularly in worship.
7. Maurice curses and uses God's name in vain in order to be "tough."
8. Rob reads his Bible daily.
9. Shawn has held a grudge for years.
10. Alicia always tries to speak up for someone who is being slandered.

E.

Learn to spell these words. Use as many as you can in three sentences.

regeneration   salvation   condemnation   gracious   contrition   repentance

23
The Office of the Keys

A.

Fill in the missing words.

The Lord Jesus gave to His church on earth the O_____ of the
K_____. He b_____ on His disciples and said to them,
"R_____ the H_____ S_____. If you f_____ anyone his s_____, they
are f_____ ; if you do not f_____ them, they are not f_____."
Our Lord, then, gave this special a_____ to His c_____ on earth.
These powers are the right to p_____ the Gospel, to administer the
S_____, and to f_____ sins and to w_____ forgiveness from
the i_____ . A congregation exercises this power when it c_____ a
pastor and delegates to him the authority to exercise publicly the keys given by the
C_____ to the c_____. This work of preaching, teaching, and caring for
souls in the congregation is known as the holy m_____, and the pastors
who serve are doing so in the name of C_____.

B.

Your congregation has a pastor (or pastors) who serve(s) the church in the name of Christ.
Supply the missing information.

My pastor is the Reverend _____. He was called to our congregation in _____ (year) and was installed on _____(month–day–year). He has
served _____ years as shepherd of our flock.

My pastor is the Reverend _____. He was called to our
congregation in _____ (year) and was installed on _____(month—day—year).
He has served _____ years as shepherd of our flock.

1. He preaches the Gospel on these public occasions:

   _____ _____ _____

2. He administers Holy Baptism about _____ times a year. He administers Holy
   Communion about _____ times a year to about _____ persons.

3. When the Lord's Supper is celebrated, he pronounces the Absolution to the communicants in these words: (*Lutheran Worship*, p. 137 or 158).

   _____

   _____

   _____

C.

Write these words before the definitions to which they are related.

penitent   impenitent   repent   remit sin   retain sin   exclude a sinner   absolve a sinner

_____ 1. tell those who are not sorry for their sins that they may not approach the Lord's Table until they repent

_____ 2. feel no sorrow for one's sins

_____ 3. tell sinners that God has forgiven them

_____ 4. forgive sin

_____ 5. turn from sin to grace

_____ 6. withhold forgiveness

_____ 7. realize your sin and ask forgiveness

D.

Write 1, 2, 3, or 4 before each sentence to indicate which step of church discipline is being followed.

_____ The Christian congregation decides that an impenitent sinner was no longer a member entitled to Holy Communion or other privileges of the church unless he or she repents.

_____ Three members of the congregation went to speak to a member who had sinned grievously and was not repentant.

_____ An impenitent sinner was invited to attend a church meeting to be admonished because of his or her impenitence.

_____ A member went to a fellow member to reprove him or her for a serious sin and impenitence.

E.

Write yes before those sentences which tell of love, honor, and service toward the pastor.
Write no before those which tell of disrespect and lack of service.

_____ 1. Amber prayed that her pastor would have a large adult confirmation class.

_____ 2. Daniel and his friends agreed to help the pastor by getting all things ready for confirmation instruction.

_____ 3. Shortly before confirmation instruction began, Shontay turned on her portable CD player.

_____ 4. A group of boys are known to make fun of their pastor because he is elderly.

_____ 5. Mika and her friends laughed and giggled so much during the sermon that the pastor had to stop and look in their direction.

_____ 6. Mr. Haggett always addresses his pastor with respect and kindness.

_____ 7. Mrs. Evans doesn't want to invite an unchurched person to church; she says, "That's the pastor's job."

_____ 8. When Thai hears a sermon that helps him a lot he thanks the pastor.

_____ 9. Mrs. McMahon spoke up for her pastor when she heard a friend criticize him.

F.

Learn to spell these words. Use as many as you can in four sentences.

penitent   impenitent   pastor   absolve   excommunicate   ministry   congregation

24
Confession and Absolution

A.

Join the correct sentence halves by writing the numbers of the sentence beginnings before the endings that complete the thought.

1. The two parts of Confession are

2. We must confess all sins

3. To our pastor we may confess

4. Our pastor will not reveal

5. It is a good plan to consult

6. When the pastor speaks the Absolution he

7. Forgiveness granted by the pastor

____ before God.

____ the secret matters told to him in consultation.

____ confessing our sins and receiving forgiveness.

____ frequently with our pastor

____ those sins which we know and feel in our hearts.

____ holds true in heaven also.

____ forgives sin in the name of God.

B.

In making a confession we should examine ourselves according to the Ten Commandments.
Write the number of commandments against which each of these people sinned.

____ 1. Ricardo carries a secret grudge against the boy who told on him.

____ 2. Kris says "honest to God!" to convince others that she is telling the truth.

____ 3. Gina envies the girl who gets new clothes more often than she does.

____ 4. Jonathan deliberately thinks impure and lustful thoughts.

____ 5. When Michael was sick, he said, "I'll make it through by myself." He did not ask God for health or strength.

____ 6. Jana is paid by the hour, but she is known to idle on the job.

____ 7. Though he can well afford to give much more, Reggie gives about 1 percent of his income to church and charity.

____ 8. Mariana is always complaining about the faults of others.

____ 9. Stephan refers to his parents as, "My old man and my old lady."

C. *Special Exercises*

1. Memorize the confession of sins used in your congregation's worship services (see *Lutheran Worship*, p. 136 or p. 158).

2. With what words does the pastor admonish the congregation to confess sins?

_____

_____

_____

_____

3. Why does the hymnal suggest that the people kneel for the confession?

_____

_____

_____

_____

D.

Who made a confession of sins in each of these cases?

2 Samuel 12:13 _____ Who was his confessor? _____

1 Samuel 7:3–6 _____ Who was their confessor? _____

Daniel 9:1–19 _____

Luke 15:11–24 _____ To whom did he confess? _____

E.

Learn to spell these words. Use them in a sentence.

confession   absolution

25

The Sacrament
of the Altar

A.

Write the endings to these sentences.

1. The Sacrament of the Altar was instituted by _____.
2. The words of institution for Holy Communion were recorded in Holy Scriptures by _____, _____, _____, and _____.
3. Our Lord Jesus Christ instituted the Holy Supper on the same_____

   _____
4. The visible elements in the Lord's Supper are _____ and _____.
5. In the Lord's Supper we receive the body of Christ in, with, and under the

   _____ .
6. At the Lord's Table Christ's blood is given us in, with, and under the _____.
7. "Mass" is a very ancient name for the _____ _____.

B.

Read each Bible reference and write a title that summarizes what happened on the night the Sacrament was instituted.

Mark 14:12–16 _____   John 13:21–30 _____

_____   _____

Luke 22:14–22 _____   Matthew 26:36–46 _____

_____   _____

Luke 22:31–34 _____   Matthew 26:47–56 _____

_____   _____

John 13:1–17_____

_____

C.

Show that each of these statements is true by copying brief phrases from the words of institution to prove your point.

1. The true body of Christ is present in, under, and with the bread.

   _____

2. The true blood of Christ is present in, under, and with the wine.

   _____

3. All communicants are to take both bread and wine.

   _____

4. Holy Communion brings forgiveness of sins.

_____

5. Christians should attend the Lord's Supper regularly.

_____

D.

Follow the directions of each statement.

1. If the bread and wine are changed into the body and blood, circle B. If not, circle R.   B   R
2. If Holy Communion is a "sacrifice" of Christ's body, circle R. If not, circle E.   R   E
3. If it is wrong to adore the bread, circle M. If not, circle E.   M   E
4. If the body and blood of Christ are received with the bread and wine, circle I. If not, circle A.   I   A
5. If the Bible tells us that the body and blood are truly present, circle S. If not, circle K.   S   K
6. If the bread and wine merely "represent" the body and blood of Christ, circle I. If not, circle S.   I   S
7. If the Lord's Supper is a means of grace, circle I. If not, circle N.   I   N
8. If Christ intended the wine only for the ministers to drink, circle G. If the congregation is to receive the wine, too, circle O.   G   O
9. If the Lord's Supper is only a "memorial feast," circle O. If it is that and more, circle N.   O   N
10. If *transubstantiation* means "changed into," circle O. If not, circle F.   O   F
11. If Jesus instituted the Lord's Supper during the Passover meal, circle F. If not, circle B.   F   B
12. If Holy Communion is a testament in which Jesus gives Himself, circle S. If it is not, circle R.   S   R
13. If "often" means that we should partake of the Sacrament only four times a year circle E. If not, circle I.   E   I
14. If you can reject the Lord's Supper and still be a Christian, circle A. If not, circle N.   A   N
15. If you are convinced that the Lord's Supper is the true body and blood of the Lord Jesus for believers to eat and drink, circle S. If not, circle D.   S   D

E.

Write these words beneath the correct pictures. Use a dictionary if you are not sure of the meaning. Host, flagon, chalice, paten

F.

Learn to spell these words. Use them in five sentences.

evangelist   disciple   remission   paten   Communion
communicant   remembrance   altar   flagon   host   Eucharist   chalice

26
Benefits, Power, and Use of the Lord's Supper

A.
Write yes if the statement is true and no if it is false.

_____ 1. When we receive the Lord's Supper in faith, we receive forgiveness of sins, life, and salvation.

_____ 2. If we have forgiveness of sins, we also have life and salvation.

_____ 3. Holy Communion is the only way we can receive true forgiveness.

_____ 4. The word *communion* implies a "oneness of faith."

_____ 5. The real benefits of the Lord's Supper rest in the act of eating and drinking.

_____ 6. We receive forgiveness of sins through the Sacrament as we trust Christ's words, "Given and shed for you for the remission of sins."

_____ 7. *Fasting* means "not eating."

_____ 8. It is wrong to fast and prepare for the Lord's Supper.

_____ 9. A communicant is unworthy if he or she does not believe in the Real Presence and the forgiveness offered by Christ.

_____ 10. A person with a weak faith may attend Holy Communion.

B.
Write three questions that Christians may ask when examining themselves for Holy Communion.

1. _____

_____

2. _____

_____

3. _____

_____

C.
Place a check (✓) before those who may receive the Lord's Supper.

___ 1. An unbeliever

___ 2. A condemned criminal who has repented

___ 3. A baptized baby

___ 4. One who thinks that the bread and wine merely represent Christ's body and blood

___ 5. A repentant believer on his deathbed

___ 6. A believer who has lost consciousness on her deathbed

___ 7. A church member who carries a grudge

___ 8. A repentant believer who has no good clothes to wear

___ 9. A neatly dressed believer who has not examined himself or herself

___ 10. A scoffer

___ 11. A believer who feels for his or her sins and "hungers and thirsts for righteousness"

___ 12. A church member who has no intention of following Christ in daily life

D.

Tell why each of these does not show the proper attitude toward the Sacrament of the Altar.

1. A young woman spent an hour on Sunday morning fixing her hair and pressing her dress in preparation for approaching the Lord's Table, but she spent no time in spiritual preparation.

2. A man said that where he came from everybody received Communion only once a year during Holy Week.

3. Hayley maintains that the Bible sets four times per year as the maximum for Communion attendance.

4. A young man attends Communion once a year because, "If I don't, they will take my name off the church record."

5. Samantha believes that if she goes to Communion every time the Lord's Supper is celebrated she would be overdoing a good thing.

6. Ramon fears that if he communes too frequently others may think he's trying to be too saintly.

7. In a certain congregation, all except those who intend to commune leave the church service right after the offering, before the distribution of the Lord's Supper.

E.

1. Confirmation is a rite of profession in the church. *Complete these three sentences telling what you will do at your confirmation.*

    a. I will publicly affirm m_____ b_____ v_____.

    b. I will make public confession of m_____ f_____.

    c. I shall be received into c_____ m_____ of my
       c_____.

2. At your confirmation you promise to be loyal to your faith and church. Experience teaches that some fall away from the faith. *Draw a cross (+) before those things you will want to do to stay in the faith.*

    ___ a. Pray without ceasing

    ___ b. Attend church at least once a week

    ___ c. Read your Bible regularly

    ___ d. Be active in church work

    ___ e. Give proportionately for the support of your congregation

    ___ f. Attend the Lord's Supper regularly

    ___ g. Give generously for mission work

    ___ h. Tell others of Christ and His great love

    ___ i. Keep the Ten Commandments ever before your eyes

    ___ j. Ask the Holy Spirit to make your faith strong and living

F.

Learn to spell these words. Use them in two sentences.

confirmation   rite   vow   covenant